Ethiopian Aliens

Poems

Clesirdia Nzorozwa

Mwanaka Media and Publishing Pvt Ltd,
Chitungwiza, Zimbabwe

*

Creativity, Wisdom, and Beauty

Publisher: *Mmap*
Mwanaka Media and Publishing Pvt Ltd
24 Svosve Road, Zengeza 1
Chitungwiza, Zimbabwe
mwanaka@yahoo.com
mwanaka13@gmail.com
https://www.mmapublishing.org
www.africanbookscollective.com/publishers/mwanaka-media-and-publishing
https://facebook.com/MwanakaMediaAndPublishing/

Distributed in and outside N. America by African Books Collective
orders@africanbookscollective.com
www.africanbookscollective.com

ISBN: 978-1-77933-142-7
EAN: 9781779331427

© CLERSIDIA NZOROZWA 2024

All rights reserved.
No part of this book may be reproduced or transmitted in any form or by any means, mechanical or electronic, including photocopying and recording, or be stored in any information storage or retrieval system, without written permission from the publisher

DISCLAIMER
All views expressed in this publication are those of the author and do not necessarily reflect the views of *Mmap*.

Table of contents

Don't forget
BLACK!
Afrika
Throw the bones
Soldier on soldier
My homeland
Strip Africa Naked
To whom it may concern
Heaven on earth
Breathing
The slums
PURPOSE
Umbrella minds
Lord
Unborn problem
Emergency
Cries
I Am a Hero
Eyes of the streets
TROUBLED WATERS
Dear outside world……
WRITEN LETTER
UNSAID PRAYERS
Ten to five stitches
253
Halo Maid
Hiccups

UNDERSTAND
Tell me
I'M NOT THE ONE FOR YOU
UNCONDITIONAL LOVE
POISONOUS BEAUTIFUL SNAKE
HE IS
Where have you been?
Him and Her
I feel love
Furnace!
Ours
COLORLESS RAINBOW
True to the heart
We can love a little
Dodo
Virgin Mary
Only survivor
No Heart Beat
All that's left
Don't
Remember Me
I do
Listen
Stand By
LET IT GO
Never
Come by the tree
PUBLIC TOILET
Primrose
Purpose
DESTINY

Blank Pages
In and out
16
Blue
Mmap New African Poets Series

Introduction note

Many of the pieces in this book are from my experience, going through life we meet and part ways with a lot of people, events Emotions, we learn to shield, we get hardened by certain encounters, we become defensive in every form, have fun riding through this emotional roller-coaster. If need be please have a wiper close to you incase you feel heavy and need a release.

As you flip through the book some of these pieces are fictional and imaginative pieces like *Strip Africa Naked, Ethiopian Aliens, Soldier on Soldier*, these pieces were inspired by our own African history, being an African young woman from Zimbabwe I grew up reading books on black empowerment.

I grew up in Chitungwiza, it's a big ghetto town where a lot of young people are exposed to a lot of things such as drugs, with poor standards of living. You will notice pieces such as the slums, to whom it may concern speak deeply about my home town

Have fun and enjoy every piece, dig for all the literal devices, have your own meaning and understanding to each and every poem.

Special thanks to Tendai Mwanaka,

People of smoke,

1zwi Poetry.

Don't forget

Hey brother!!!

Chest to Chest!
Fists in the air!
Chants of oneness filled the air!
At the forefront we marched,
So one of us might become the heir,
The heir to the throne of the leopards!
Red eyes from the rising smoke, Breath slow so you don't choke.
At the fore front we stood in dignity, honor and with firmness.
With firmness so not only that one of us could live lavishly,
For In our veins the blood of oneness flows.

Hey sister!
Remember the Caves our mothers said to hide.
Remember how you, I and the jungle became one.
Like a wedded couple,
Come rain come thunder,
The fleas we shall squander!
The bitter pills we shall swallow.
But now why act shallow?
Have you forgotten the oath we took in the jungle?
It was an empty one I hear the rivers mumble.

BLACK!

To them Ethiopia is a home for Aliens,
Flooded with gold gods named it, ELDERADO
Ask my other brother from another mother, he hardly knows his dictionary well
But he told me to tell you if you ask me what Ethiopia and to be Ethiopian means.
Right before a cooper bullet flew right through his brains he told me to tell you
We are from the soil, the ones who toil, who rest only when their bones turn to foil.
I remember very well as my skittish self I let every single word sink in right to the core of my bone marrow
He said there deep within our black tents flows the red fluid but ours is black,
Check the DNA the little cells smile, sweat and cry 'we are black, we are strong, and we are the sons of ABRAHAM'
Men of honor not ruffians
My mother's cook peace in huge clay pots
They pour in the Zambezi for the spirits of peace to protect the man whose heart is black
The elderly serve sweet brew for our ancestors patched throats to swallow
The roots that's what defines a real traditional man of the caliber
Our pride rest in the great melanin
We are black, from the soil, the ones who toil and no man has a better definition of BLACK!

Afrika

She has been crying all along
Finally she sings the songs of joy
Laughter echoes from deep within her heart
Children now sing along to the songs of their mothers
No more shall they sing the songs of woe
So much talent and wisdom
The power of a black man
The mountains smiled
The rivers tell of the stories
When it used to rain blood
When the birds were silenced
Never to sing again for the cries of a woman in labor become the song, day in and day out
Painful the cries of Africa
To drink from the springs once more
To drink from the living waters that brings nothing but happiness
Never shall it rain lava that burnt your beautiful dark skin
Never shall you be troubled by the fleas
For the dark shadows have been seized at the command of the man who loves you so dearly

Throw the bones

Read aloud the pros and cons
The future holds uncertainty
A cloud of fire might emerge
Huff and puff on the pipe
Blow ashes so they fall blind
Blind on which crooked path I have taken
Palms together under the bushy shady tree
That's where my forefathers await for me
They await my prayers and praises
To the umkhulu khulu they shall deliver
Deliver on my behalf for he is a keeper

Look from the south marches an army
An army of whirl winds
It carries with it deformed images
Could it be the gods of the night the ancestors talk of?
Run to the Sangoma for a little bit of pick me up
You fool!
Darkness never conquers darkness
The one who is greater only gets to command the rebellious
The Sangoma is the father of all unclean spirits
But Elders said he shall cleanse the who village
Is cleansing really cleansing of the spirit and soul?
Does it mean he is only binding his own rebellious spirits?
The wind carries nothing but darkness
Ran to the invincible God, he shall become visible unto you with time
Eyes deep with your heart shall be opened to see the light
He knows all the pros and cons

Open the book of peace
Read aloud the holy wars
The past holds nothing but fear, pain and sorrow
A cloud of heavy, pure springs might sprung up
Praise and worship on the cross
Blow some kisses so they open their eyes
Open their eyes on why you never stumble

Soldier on soldier

When he got hit, I lost a limb.
At that moment that's when I heard a voice calling my name.
There was a little light that blocked my vision
With a smile on my face, I thought so this must be heaven.

And this voice, this voice, could it be God almighty's voice?
Well back on earth nobody knew what he sounded like except for
Moses and the Israelites 'THURNDER, RUMBLING, LIGHTINING!
Suddenly anger had hit me; he had to know the world he created was full of chaos.
I was going to tell him,
I tried to raise my arm.
I felt numb.
I couldn't feel my body.
I tried to scream but it was pointless.
That's when I thought if I was really in heaven and if this was God and his seraphim's surrounding me and back on earth people said,
God can read minds and hear people's thoughts, I started to pray in my heart.
I was in the battle field,
Fighting for my people,
Fighting for freedom,
I only wish to know, you were seeing all this from up here?
I lost a friend in the swamps.
He got hit; the last I saw of him was the skittish expression on his face.
The blood that oozed out from his mouth and noise, before he fell on his face

I saw blurry visions of strong man with scary ugly faces.
I only wish to know why you choose me instead of my wounded dying friend.
You should have taken us both to this paradise!

The light remained constant; it caused me this sharp pain like someone was pocking my eyes from the inside.
That's when I realized maybe it was all pointless.
I mean, who was I to think that God would listen to a sinner like me.
I buster red into tears, I should have listened to Amai and Baba.
They told me to stay in hiding, but No!
I wanted to fight side by side with my friend,
I wanted to be a hero like my friend's Uncle,
Maybe raise the family name from the dust,
I wanted to die in honor,
I wanted………

Then I heard my brother's voice calling me.
I noticed him coming from the East.
He held my hand and said 'we shall fight for honor, we shall fight indignity, and we shall fight side by side.'
Then he disappeared into the tall grass.
My vision became clearer, that's when I realized I was still lying in the swamps.
I looked aside in shame; men never shed tears, not from Africa.
I smelled something like rotten meat; I spotted the body that was lying right beside me.
It was him, my hero, my brother, he was dead!

They helped me to sit up straight, I noticed Amai running like a tortoise coming from the north, with her right hand pressed against her back.
She screamed 'it's over!'
'The war is over!'
I sobbed bitterly……………

My homeland

Sweat more because you are black and that's worth more than a million thoughts of an idle man.
Susana a mother of five,
She never cried bitterly when her husband died,
She could buy the world with her sweat.

Feed her cubs from her own sweat and blood,
She could have been the next billionaire.
Go against the odds,
A man in her nature!

She wore Diamonds and pearls on the funeral,
She was among the Elderly men with beards,
She faced her fears of being poor decades ago.

What is a man?
The one with a voice that threatens to murder the eardrums?
The one with blisters in his palms?
Or is it the one that slaves always in the sun, day in and day out with no sleep at all?

Indeed in the eyes of the society she was a disgrace,
A freak of nature, an alien although in the eyes of her husband she was a priceless jewel and to her children a heroin.
In her mother's eyes she was a mere cub grown to be a jaguar!

Earning the title mama Africa,
Although times were hard she kept playing her cards.

Work ethics, play the chase game well,
Learnt even from her rivals so now she is an icon,
Even her rivals now marvel at her feet.
The statue of struggle and strength!

Welcome to the land of milk and honey
Where hard work enslaves all for the fear of poverty motivates all.
Welcome to the land of dreams
Africa is rich and a small piece of dirt can give men plenty to feed.

Strip Africa Naked

Pimp, pimp, white teeth, red lips, yellow cheeks, pink hair
Orange thighs, black heels, charcoal feet in white heels
African Barbie Doll

Chin up, Chin up, chest out
Those round pumpkins from the heart of Africa
Bring them out!
Catwalk, talk slow, piggy accent, mini skirt,
Don't be naïve red Indians love flat bellies.
Forget about African Attires, your body is Africa.
Let's strip her naked, let them see what you are made of
African Barbie Doll

Step on their toes with heels; greet them with plastic gloves on.
Don't forget to wear that plastic smile, hold your breath when they try to hug
Old women in patched African Attires, Kitchens with smoke make my eyes water
I can't stand the cow dung and the hens, the dog chewed on my shoe.
But you are Africa, the son of the soil.
The sons and daughters of Nehanda and Kaguvi
African Barbie Doll

What happened to you Africa!!!
I used to beautiful; they told me yellow bones get a thousand likes!
Walk half, it attracts
Tell your fellow charcoal brothers and sisters to stand in line for the bleaching movie

Long artificial nails make you the boss
Knees and thighs sell out here!!!
They never told me rotten meat attracts a lot of flies
Our fallen Aunts told me
'Beautiful roses with colorful, big and bright petals attract a lot of bees'
The red Indians only helped us to strip Africa naked!!!
African Barbie Doll

No more sitting around the fire, chewing on roasted peanuts.
Passing around the wooden plate, because brotherhood is what our mothers taught us.
I thought when they said history "past", meant follow, copy and paste his-story and her-story,
Make it your own story, carry the pride of Africa in the way you dress and talk child.
Short hair, black as ebony, melanin popping, African Attires, Ancient Queens
Zindwe the daughter of Ndwandwe, the chief of Mashabana, the wife of King Lobengula
And a mother to our brothers and sisters, she resembled Africa.
A tell to be passed on from generation to generation
Not it's how these Baboons, Barbarians used to live in the past, we came with civilization.

They told me times change, this is yet another era.
Does our barbaric and savage ways have to change, from covering the pride of Africa to show more booty and boobs?
Does how we walk, talk, greet elders and the color of our skins have to change from melanin to yellow to piggy pink then white?

Red Indians killed our mothers and Aunts, gave us modern satellite twenty first century artificial ones
Aunts with plastic faces, they all look alike
Angels because they are from china's 'plastic'
Demons because they talk more plastic, stretch marks are out of fashion,
Pink hair is trending, no pimples, Botox for these wrinkles.
They enter the oven; they come out looking like clowns
They helped us to strip Africa naked
She joined the stripers club, she is one of them now.

To whom it may concern

Hardly received any mail!
I did, had a thought about it,
Well! Probably the government was too broke to employ postman.
Or is it, it couldn't afford to buy motor cycles; there was indeed a cash crisis.
Walking home deep in thoughts,
Reminiscining on how my jobless, stressful life would go about in this country.
My throat felt rusty and rather dry.
Fortunately I found a piece of silver and a marble stone.
I threw them in the air hopping they would fall right back in my rough dirty hands in a pothole full of sewage, I watched them disappear into the green slim water.
Well I smiled, looked around, playfully bent as my hands dived into the rescue,
'My precious silver' I licked it clean

Presenting it to the old lady whose smile brightened the day of every little kid my age,
Although she had several missing teeth, she didn't mind sharing a good joke and a pleasant laugh with one or two customers.
The gossip ladies advised to stay away from her; they told stories on how she swallowed her own womb
The missing teeth were evident enough to prove their stories true.

Even though 'survivor' sent Lorries of groceries but never dared to set his foot on her compound.
The clean patched clothe tied around her head and another tied around her waist, she bitterly sang war songs.

At times she found comfort in the foreign religious songs, she said they reminded her of her foreign priest friend who kept her strong and steadfast in prayer.
Despite being stripped off of her African pride by the so called land owner who sexually abused her on the farm, she worked on as a maid years ago.

She was a woman of the culture, ancient in her own fashion.
A warrior in her own time, a savage in her own prime
Not a worrier, a true symbol of faith and a pillar of strength.
The gossip ladies wore the modern fashion like a dog collar.

Taking pride in which they did not know,
If their tongues knew better they could have bitten them off.
Maybe spit out that which killed all the old woman's cats,
If their heads would take pride in the clothes African woman tied around their heads covering their ears so to fall short of what goes on under other soul's roofs.

Maybe their shaven, platted, weaved empty heads would learn of what it means to be an African woman.
If their hands knew better than laughing hard, they could have asked for guidance in this world of 'women better start earning a living or you might lose your husband to his secretary,'
Maybe their weak hearts would have learned of what the African cultures and the bibles teaches on how to keep your head down and letting your husbands be husbands.

Well Whipped my smelly hands clean on my patched tiny almost crop top t shirt.
Gracefully purchased, and licked joyfully to my money's worth,

What more can a human being need on a sunny day except for a nice sweet homemade ice loll.
It was so good it made my taste buds tingle

Heaven on earth

Oh God how I love to go shopping by the garbage place the food is cheap there!
Where I live my landlord the rats hardly ask for their rent.
In the swamps where there is less noise,
Less killing and blood,
Less chit chatter and gossips,
You should see how the rich man's wife roams around bragging about the diamond rings and necklaces,
How they scream on the sight of men like me.
The Unfairness of God!
What they call garbage is breakfast and dinner,
Trust me I have seen tables full.
They eat like gods and are as fat as pigs,
The fleas have abandoned me for my veins have dried up.
The cockroaches hate me, for it has been a million years ever since they had a Christmas.
The cockroaches in their homes have coats that are shiny,
The rats surely have to party every weekend, Food is never scarce.
But my rags don't fit no more; I'm a dead man that walks the earth,

The rich have no pity,
They have named me after their stray dogs.
They told their children to run and hide from the street monsters.
They tell them we cursed our mothers,
But I heard about the poor and heaven won't there be greedy, ugly, fat men there too?
What is my purpose to life?
Dig in the dirt and argue with mice and rats?
Heaven on earth is a dream I have always had,

But the world is so unfair others are born you live lavishly while others suffer.

Breathing

The wind came houses fell to the ground
The storm roared trees fell no sound
But I'm still breathing
In the bottomless pit I fell
Family and friends gave up on telling my tales
But I'm still breathing

From the sky I fell to hit the ground head first
A few bumps heroes don't cry.
Yes I'm still breathing

Crumbs of bread and a drop of milk
Empty pots with boiling water
I Say my prayers before supper
Hoping the water would change into bread and butter
Look at what Jesus did at the wedding in Canaan

But like no other warrior
I'm a true knight
The Holy Spirit my sword
No matter the weather
Life goes on, it don't matter
Grateful even though it's painful
But I'm still breathing

The slums

Slimy little world
Under the card board where it feels warmer
She sleeps and dreams "heaven can never be any better"

Torn clothes in winter they are warm
Rainy days our cardboard homes stand firm
Like toads in the muddy water we sleep

The streets are safe
Stray dogs are our friends
When the darkness comes we hug
The trees
They always rock us to sleep

Mother moon said never to be afraid of the shadows
For she gave birth to an army
An army of millions of brothers and sisters to watch over you and me

Food is scarce
That's the new anthem for the rats and mice
The ants taught us food hoarding
Survival of the fittest, it's a jungle out here

In a tiny hole we live
It's never too little every mouth and stomach is always full
Only these skeletons tell the truth
My sisters are no longer curvy

PURPOSE

Oh Lord, dear Lord taking every word in.
I swallow the pill every single day,
I have prayers written down in rows and columns.
On the walls, on the ceiling and I craved them on the floor too.
You know I can never say them,
My lips have been sealed for years.
I have thousands of sins committed all in 24hours multiply by my age.
My colors are red and black,
Black blend with my heart, my spirit and soul,
Black is the blood that I write prayers with on the walls.
My skin is covered in red,
Red little letters that say you shall burn.
My right hand is curved with an iron pin little fleshy words that say
'repent you serpent'
What is my purpose?
To serve like a little demon that destroys hearts?
What is my purpose and destiny?

Oh Lord God!!
I love them all; I'm obsessed with them all,
I can never get enough.
Peter is kind, Johnny is tall, Joseph is rich, and I just can't decide, who I should be with?
Lord! Your word on adultery, your word on Lust, Your word on harlotry,
It has fallen on deaf ears.
Hosea and his harlot, Am I the second version of her?

Who can be the Hosea?
Prudence!
He knows about them all, he knows my heart is divided,
And I'm a woman of purity but still walk in the shadows of the woman that rule the night.
Fate and destiny!
Who am I?
What is my purpose and destiny?
To have whosoever I please and still be labeled the prophetess?

Umbrella minds

He swallowed the syllabus only to vomit failure.
Laughter congratulated him with a slap of shame in public,
Dishonored from the family,
The high status quo got disrupted so it spat on his face like he was an alien.

The toothless syllabus left deep wounds in his heart,
Words burnt his high spirited soul to dust.
The family name fell from the tree top hitting the ground head first.
The fierce father lion chewed on the stupid results slip and swallowed it like a chunk of meat.

Mother hen ate all her unhatched rotten eggs,
Fear of giving birth to brainless - bookworms had hit her brain waves.
My precious saw less shoes, patched special jean were thrown at the center of the city,
With a half-moon smile the world spat on my face.

He ran into the night with only his shadow beside him,
It smiled at him,
It hugged him still, even though the world had become a bitter pill to swallow.
The cruel wind rocked him to sleep,
That's when he saw the angry moon in his sleep.

He bowed down in terror,
Then a voice said _"bless you son"_ then he woke up,
A priest with a bible in his hand stood before him.

He held out his hand and the poor boy took it.
Raised to his feet again!
Hope to relive again!

He whispered
'Umbrella minds never ran out of ideas'
God is a genetic genius,
He has an umbrella mind so know there are still time and many doors to be opened.
Stay in the right path, where there is no way for God, there is a door way
Umbrella minds!

Lord

For the pain,
For the grief,
For the love,
For the life,
For the tears,
May the lord come!

The power of will,
The power of wisdom,
The power of heavens,
The power of thoughts,
The power of visions,
May the lord come!

Wait for the rains,
May the storm pass!
Wait for the rains,
May the violent wind pass!
Wait for the rains,
May the lord come!

Elements of life,
Elements of death,
Elements of pain,
Elements of sorrow,
Elements of joy,
May the lord come?

Sit I will and Think still.

Walk still and Talk still.
Lie still and meditate still.
Look still and understand still.
Life just like a candle, it will never last!
May the lord come?

Unborn problem

36 weeks…
Ululations of tears!
Tremble away yours fears.
The outside is a monster.
Ready or not, ready or not!
Push! Problem was born.

42 weeks….
Sandstorms that choke,
Smile away your tears.
Open eyes drop,
Ready or not, ready or not!
Cheese! Plastic smile was born.

497 weeks…
Love came, stayed then left.
Laugh away your rusty memories.
Into the womb mine shall return.
Far from the breasts it rest.
Too old a man, gums know no teeth.

Swallow mine back.
Into your womb!
No bullets fired, it knows no war.
Swallow it back.
Into your waist,
Lock me up in the silence of your fears.
Bring me not into this jungle.

Ready or not, ready or not!
Vomited into a big pond,
Small were the fins.
Fishing hooks and pirates.
Throw it, hold it.
Swim to the surface.

A bottle with pirates,
Paradise in silence,
Isolation no violence,
Ready or not, ready or not!
A bomb woke my soul.
To never dream of such beauty!
A life in a bottle!
With a boat of dead pirates,
Entrance like the eye of a needle,
Surface way too peaceful!

Ready or not, ready or not!
This miracle we live in.
Dream of all the solutions,
Come forth not in this day and age.
A few more years before the waters break.
Your cry shall be our freedom.
This is my letter to you,
Unborn child!

Emergency

It's on the way!
The wind carriers the wails,
Wails of pain and joy, impatience struck me like lighting.
It was indeed overdue but now it says so long to hiding.
It knocks on the door; it screams "The strong shall prevail!"

Let thy will be done, let thy Glory shine.
When will the lord come, when will the wild repent?
Let thy will be done, let thy Glory shine.
When will the tears shed be remembered?
Or was it all in vain!

Wolves dance and sing "Hallelujah the prophecy has been fulfilled"
It opened its mouth enabled through its nostrils and cried to the new long life,
Stars fell from the sky and the moon's heart was filled with songs.

"Emergency Room "souls sing it like a funeral dirge,
O' red lights blink, Zimbabwe was my side fling,
She is with child now, was it not there was a thing.
O' white lights blink, Zimbabwe is now free she named the emergency child "freedom"
Is it not the name of an ancestor you cows slaughtered?

Cries

How does it feel when your hard work is never appreciated?
When you know you have put your all in it
And still feel there is this hole in your heart
This emptiness, this plain feeling
And words can't seem to escape from your lips
That moment when you can't say it in words
Instead you let your tears tell the stories of your struggles
Your body still shakes from the anger but you still cannot express it
It still hurts you more when they are still judging you from your past
Prejudices, day in and day out
Never dared to try and understand you
Never scared that your soul might die from their hash words
A blade cuts through your heart
Every time you set your eyes on them
Their Lips are sealed and instead they let their eyes throw sharp knives instead
You Wish to just disappear, and never to be found
You curse the day you were born
Curse the world for helping you grow up
Pray never to understand a word they say to you

I Am a Hero

Silence!
Birds dare to sing on my funeral
Took off the ring before the storm came
Was once full of life like the springs
The green tree stood in isolation
But never will it loose hope
No! Not now or ever
One day I shall be with my fathers
Birds will miss these branches
Lions will miss this shed
The soil will miss my strong roots
The sun smiles from above
And the wind is glad
As it moves from about
Red or black the flag shall be raised
As if I were no hero
As if I never saved them from the wrath of the sun
As if I never saved them from hunger
I shall never be remembered of
Memories of me are lost in the flames
Eroded by the laughter of children
As they sing along to the songs of winter
Like a mulberry tree
I will shoot up in the air and this time FOR REVENGE
U shall never taste thy fruits neither shall you rest on thy shed
I am remembered when they are hungry
I am remembered when they are sweating
I am remembered in the cold winters

Only to be forgotten when the axe men pay me a visit in the dark night
Revenge is never the best way to make them remember
But at least they would feel the pain I feel
At least they will know how hard it is never to be appreciated for who you are
They will know what it is to feel worthless
When u once thought and was told you are special
Shall be the pain in their hearts
Thorns that never let them dance to the tunes in their mind, a proud hero
Whom they shall never salute
Die a proud hero
Whom they shall never remember

Eyes of the streets

Eyes red like pepper…
She walks about to the center of the city
Clothed in purple…
Walks about to the center of the temple

Ecstasy…
Kept her eyes open till broad day light
The inner woman confess
'No it was the gas pipe

Exhausted…
Crawls to the neighbors doorstep
'My wife is not bringing income another day'

Half moon smile…
The seven spirits now celebrate
'We shall make this bull plough our seven fields'

A damsel in red…
'Let me pet you while you wait on the Queen's arrival.'
Proverb scriptures are forgotten
Her eyes revealed to the bull the unspoken pleasures

Clothed in innocence…
She walks about to the center of the city
Robe as white as snow…
She walks about to the center of the temple
Prophecies unfolded, secrets are untold

Written on her outer garments…
'Woman of peace, love and faith'
Inner garments as filthy as slim

As rotten as a carcass
The outer look deceives many
Purity is in the eyes of the beholder

Spirituality shall have many garments unfolded
Humanity is nothing without the creator
A molding of clay is easily eroded

Search deeper the inner man might be long gone
The eyes of streets see not what's deep within
An owl feeds and breeds with the hens

To the outside world
Trapped in a cocoon
In darkness I came forth
In a boat l sit still
To observe the waters that lay still
Dear Lord

Let my heart beat,
Let my mind speak,
Let my tongue taste the bitterness of your soul.
Deep within my spirit wilts.
Voices confess in front of the congress.
Truth shall undress you in front of the whole congregation!
Shame shall befall your keens man tribe,
Because of your sins the third generation shall live like rats.

Lord God father to Jesus Christ and husband to Israel turn a blind eye and a deaf ear!
You turned from a house kitten to a wild ruthless jackal,
You and God are no longer the same.
For what is men if he isn't a reflection of God?
Nothing but a molding of clay!!!
To the soil you shall return,
You lack guide and truth,
You lack wisdom and will.

Let my heart beat,
Let my mind speak,
Let my tongue confess,
Like Isaiah baptize me with the finest charcoal from your heavenly furnace,
For my tongue confess nothing but lies.
And deep within the truth I locked away from judgment,
It's not my fault my spirit became one of the lost ones.
Your people father, they are sly and deceitful.
I'm only a product of everything I go through!
Your wish is my command but I'm afraid your people will judge.
I'm praying since I'm now like Sodom -Gomorrah I deserve not to burn.
Like the walls of Jericho don't burn thy temple down with tongues of fire.
It is I your one and only child,
I pray not for temptation but strength and courage to face it all!

TROUBLED WATERS

The troubled waters shake violently
An iron strong fist leaves prints
A night of tears makes me shiver and tremble in a corner
I sit as I watch the monster's Claus struggle to break in

It threatens to break right through the thick walls
To unplug the energy source cable
A cable that connects to me,
Emotions are transmitted to me

I sob from the inside
I hear voices screaming from the outside
But my vision can see as far as these walls I am trapped in
It's too quite here at times but summer never comes
I cannot keep track of time but my tinny shell tells a lot

One of these days I shall come forth

As I dream, I grow older with time
I have come to know something bigger than me is out
It has greater power…
I giggle, I blush, I smile, and I laugh,
At times I have beautiful dreams

The words come to me,
As warm as winter
As beautiful as spring
As cold as summer

The love of the one I don't know of yet
I live deep inside them
A big palm waves from the outside
I watch it go left, right then center

Its heart beats tenderly
Calmly and that's once in a blue moon
I feel at peace and thy soul dances
To the sound of thy heart beat

It never last...
Glasses breaking, the water shakes

A noisy harsh squeaky voice
Threatens to burst my eardrums

The screams get louder
I hardly get to rest father, I sob tears of blood
Fears grab my soul by the throat and threaten to choke it

But one day I shall come forth
One of these days I shall come forth
With a broken smile to cut off the endless chains of screams
One day I shall come forth with a warm winter to end the cold summer
One of these days I shall come forth with the light to end the darkness that lingers in the carriages corner

Dear outside world......

It lies on the bed...
Withered like a flower
Pale skin, sunken eyes, and dry lips
It looks like its ancestors

Shhh.......

How dare you talk like that?
It shall rise like tomorrow's sun
Bright eyes, shinny skin
Fresh like the morning due
It shall look like a new born baby

Shhh....

It cannot survive this...
Mansions and the Queen is mine for the taking
The little brats in my field they shall slave away
Like rats they shall eat from the garbage cans
Hand me the crown, since all my hair is grey
There isn't much to decide

Shhh...

Factories future lies in my hands
The maiden it loves so
The mansion is for my brats
You shall be poisoned if you wish to take possession

Shhh…

The kitchen table tells of your deeds
Let me not spill the beans
The red line you have crossed
It lays there on the metal bed helpless and hopeless
You remain the devil, you remain the selfish goddess
Its lifeline you have cut into two,
I remain the only bull with power over.

Shhh…
YOU OLD HAG!
YOU DARE ACCUSE ME OF STEALING ONE'S LIFE
FOR THESE EARTHLY PETTY LIFELESS TREASURES
WAS IT NOT ON YOUR COMMAND THAT THE DEMON
DEVOURED IT?
WAS IT NOT YOUR FATHER ON WHOSE WORDS THEY
ALL FOLLOWED?
THE LITTLE SEED ONLY HAD TO BLOOM,
YOU'RE POISON DRAINED AND LEFT IT LIFELESS,
YOUR GREED AND EGO IS WHAT I FED
A TRAITOR FROM BIRTH,
THE WORLD YOU PROMISED
I SHALL HAVE MY SHARE
IF NOT BOTH ITS BLOOD AND YOURS SHALL BE UPON
MY HEAD

SHH...
YOU SELFISH WOMAN!
WHAT DO I GET FOR BEING A HELPER

NAILING MY SOUL ON THE CROSS IS WORTH MORE THAN THESE POSSESSIONS
THE GODS SHALL TELL ON YOU

To be continued.......

WRITEN LETTER

Invisible ink print on
A life a mortal shall live
Reveal to me the chapters

In bold letters
Slowly fading in this cold weather
The story of a mortal was written
Reveal to me the chapters

The string of life
The mighty invincible umkhulu khulu holds
A pair of scissors to cut in two the molding of clay
To cut into two the ones who dance with the devil
Reveal to me the chapters

First chapters I knew not
The rest I revisit after a little slumber and fall
No magician knows not what the next chapter holds
Elevation of a downfall
Reveal to me the chapters

Picture in a frame
Define a life on a train
Events unfold, unprepared I fall
A hint or a call, so I prepare before I fall
Reveal to me the chapters

UNSAID PRAYERS

Light me that candle dear.
Place it on the table and leave me to my misery
In this cabin I was born,
In this rotten place I shall be buried in.

Don't blow the candle till midnight dear
Let it burn till the rooster cries 'IT IS TIME!'
In this farm lays my father
In this lifeless field mine will be laid

Before you leave, please hand me my mother's cloak.
Pass me my father's favorite glass and pour for me one last crunch of wine.
Hand me my sweet sister's precious bracelet
These are the only things that bring me comfort at times like these!

I must confess my sins before the clock strikes 2100
Let me wonder off into the night, I will find my way to the temple's holy gates
If the candle goes off and the roaster cries before I return, rejoice for I would have departed on a journey to reunite with my family
Dora my lovely wife, she must be waiting impatiently for my arrival
I probably deserve not thy shadow's company
Father I am a man of the darkest deeds
Me and the lovely world you created, our history share a dark chapter
I wait on your time
My heart deserve not to beat on so tenderly

I shall kneel at the temple's gates for I am a man of unclean feet
and the ground there is ever so holy
Tears shall say all my unsaid prayers
As I shall be waiting on the Lord's messengers to accompany me
on this journey

Ten to five stitches

Ma….ma…mama!
Glue for us that pattern.
There is a ball in Ethiopia.
Ought to live them fascinated!

Old garment…
Ten to five from the selvedge,
Loose stitches…
Looped loops on the seams.

Screw tight bobbin case.
That's a nymph in old fashion.
Replace the needle its blunt.
Ma…mama…
This metal is twice great grandpa's age.
It's too old a machine for this age.

Sparking thread…
20 to 10 stitches from the grain.
Ten tight stitches…
Mend my torn garment.
For the world to fall blind on nakedness!

Sparkling metal with old rusty souls,
She placed a fabric it wouldn't sew!
Two to three stitches…
Too loose to hold these pieces!
Four to five minutes…
She showed it off, spoiled princess.

Six to seven seconds…
With shame blowing her kisses,
She ran naked from the crowd holding on to the pieces.

Ma…..ma….Mama…
Ten to five from the selvedge,
It won't sew!

Tempting shinny needle,
Too young, sew me Sahara.
A new fashion for the Ball!

She placed a piece of her beneath you.
Two to three stitches…
Fasten it up quickly.
Four to five minutes…
She danced at Ball.
Crowned before my enemies!
Ma…ma…mama…
Ten to five stitches from the selvedge.
It sewed me Sahara.
New fashion the world admires!

253

This is Doctor Broken stein experiment number 250!

Grey hair, shaky legs, left foot facing backwards.
Disjointed I have been dancing with my shadow.
Waltz or waltz?
We don't need anyone!
Seven steps more.

This is experiment number 251!
White hair, broken legs, broken arms.
I have been crawl dancing with my shadow.
Broken records, broken seven steps on repeat.
Waltz or waltz?
Penny takes my hand,
Give Alone a chance.
We don't need anyone!
Seven steps more.

This is experiment number 252!
Falling white hair.
Decayed teeth, cracked lips, broken nails.
Broken folks, stinky wine, fragmented glasses.
Rusty sweet melodies,
Press play on the stereo.

I dine with my shadow!
More in your broken plate dear,
Delicious empty soup!
More in your plate sweet heart,

Delicious lonely peas cooked with pain!

This is experiment 253!
Shaved head, torn blankets,
Broken windows, cold winters,
Broken base, cracked back.
I sleep embracing my shadow.
More torn blankets!
Less shivering!
We don't need anyone.
Come into my broken arms.
Cuddle, rock yourself to sleep.

Experiments failed!
Men die alone!
Designed to never breathe alone!

Halo Maid

I peep through the little hole when you will let me in.
I see your soul dying a little slow please let me set you free.
To save you because I envy you, hold your breath don't let the poison in.
Let me be your guardian angel, follow me for tonight is the night we shall flee.

I stand here I'm a little slimy mole,
The world have rejected me,
On my cheek I have a mole,
Please remember me!

Hello Janet I'm that gardener from the slums.
I know the skin is writer poor but for your heart I have some treats.
Be my piano on your skin are written keys.
For your permission to play them right I plead.
I may not look handsome and rich but look in my heart treasures I have.
Be the first lucky maiden to explore deep within adventures I store.

I peep through the little hole on your heart and I see a storm.
I'm no magician or sorcerer but there is still hope.
Smile Maiden judge not a book by its cover.
I'm an open book with adventures unexplored so please read on.

Hiccups

Go hang if so you wish.
Is it me? I smell…
Sail the seas in a dish.
Canoes of your days you preach!

Go burr if so you wish.
Is it me? I smell a rat.
Scotching sun of Mount Everest,
The freezing daytime temperatures in the desert!
Frequently these places you visit!
Desert ever cold!
Stories never told!
Everest ever hot!
Now they preach it's odd.
Is it me? Or I smell a dead dog.

Is it my noise that got bigger?
Or the hiccups make it clearer?
The lies smell like rotten beer drink on, sewer is sweeter.
Truth is bitter.
Colorless red is a color.
Shoes for our hands in winter,
Baboons never eat dead.
Why believe what you heard?
You have seen them bake bread?
Make a fire, cook a wild cat?
Feed on dead like vulture?
Baboons of our days you teach!

Go drawn if so you wish!
Is it me? I smell burnt roses!
Black roses smile like primrose.

Desert lilies grow without a drop.
Out in the sun where it never rains.
Meadow of your days you preach.

UNDERSTAND

Understand I will.……
Cross seven oceans,
Drink the rivers dry,
So that we can fly!

Right to end of the world,
You in my arms is all I want,
Yes you are my world,
And it's you I deserve.

So please my hearts bleeds!
Understand for Adam it was Eve.
For me God created you.
Believe you me I can't breathe.

A million years until you say yes
      I shall wait on for your word.

Tell me

Hello ted!
I have a friend.
Who said you were once afraid,
To look a woman in the eyes,
And say all your lies
Like
My love is as real as colorless red.

Hi frank!
I have to be frank.
I was once in love.
Never afraid to say I love you.
Like
How I was afraid to say so long?
To look a man in the eyes
And say the truth
Like
My love is as real as grey hair on a sixty year old lad

Hey Greg
I have a friend
Who said you were once afraid
To sit with your friends at the bridge
Look them in the eyes and say all your lies
Like
I have once grabbed a woman's breasts,
They are as soft as a bag of sand

Hi clay

I have to make it clear
I was once a player
Never afraid to say to me, to several souls
Like how I was afraid to be with a player
To look a boy in the eyes
And say the truth
Like
You are my one and only
I would plant for you an off-layer tree
Since scrambled eggs are your favorite

Hi Enoch
I have a friend
Who said you were once afraid to love
To look a girl in the eyes
And say all your lies
Like I am the Greek god of love
Drink from my cup, have just but a drop
It will leave you drunk in love,
Never to fall again for another but just me

I'M NOT THE ONE FOR YOU

I'm not the one for you.
I'm not the one you should choose.
I'm the one you should loose. Degrade me, I'm not worthy.

I'm the one you should use.
Wipe your tears and fears,
Then throw away into the deep end.
Why can't you be like them?
Go ahead and take advantage!

I'm not a friend or a lover.
Save yourself, I'm a monster.
Love brings the worst out of me.
But if you keep searching deep within me there is a cave.

I'm never careful with hearts.
I might drop yours in the river of the lost souls and you might never find your way back.

UNCONDITIONAL LOVE

I am only human so when I choke from my mistakes hand me a glass of lessons so I swallow them smoothly down my sorry throat.
Hear me!
Unconditional love is the alien kind of love shared between immortals not mortals.
Let me remind you this phrase, whenever you cough out clotted blood of bloody mistakes that stink like the carcass and the misery that's been stuck down my rotten pipes,
Don't expect the world to caress you.
Sweet heart!
Unconditional love is the alien kind of love shared between immortals not mortals.
Let me remind you these words 'the world will never feel pity for you, so better swallow that bitter sweet bile as much as it stings, they are all your lessons learnt from your recklessness.
Cherish yourself!
Unconditional love is the alien kind of love shared between immortals not mortals.
Tell me!
Who do you expect to love you unconditionally?
When you can't lose yourself rationally, facially you frown when you look in the mirror you see a gorilla,
So you become artificial for the world to cherish you.

POISONOUS BEAUTIFUL SNAKE

I have the beauty that shames the mermaids.
Kings have marched into battle for my hand.
Many were slaughtered like cows for wanting to have me.
You might lose your mind if you reminisce over me.

I'm a danger to your soul and heart.
I might cut through you like a knife.
Leave scars that won't heal.
The crystal balls and to sorcerers you should appeal.

My beauty is only of the outside.
Inside I'm a dark mountain, dare not to climb.
Once you are in, I will lock you in.
You might get swallowed.

My love is that of a poisonous rose.
Be careful I might poison your heart till it becomes that of the dark lord.

HE IS

Tall and strong like the Muhacha tree.
His body covered in fur.
He is like a baboon.
Black smooth shinny skin that shames the black mamba.
When he speaks he roars like a lion.
I have never heard such a sweet and soft tone.
I'm no fool I have fallen.
Even mountains tremble down to his feet.
The deepest voice that's deeper than Mosi Oa Tunya even the Zambezi do not compare.
Large hands, long sausage fingers that can leave a hole on the wall.
He is strong like a bull with the strongest grip that of a true warrior.
I am sure he was one of Tshaka's best men.
If not he must be a warrior sent down from heaven to earth just for me.
Big eyes which resemble the round nuts in Dande,
Perfect big noise that shames the fist of Mzilikazi.
Then the black wet lips and the sweet giant's sweat on his neck you can't miss.
The ever high temperature like a volcano, his blood boils.
I have fallen, a kind heart, I'm no fool.
Perfect chest to rest my head, his body is tempting.
That's when my temperature raises, so I open my eyes with sweat on my breasts.
This was too beautiful to be true.
I wouldn't mind creating such a creature.
A molding of clay and a breath of life,
He was right beside me!

Where have you been?

Drawing pins under my feet.
I did bleed still I smiled.
I told ghosts all my secrets.
Created an imaginary friend, self-reliance!

I took solace in intimacy.
Twice a day, fourteen times per week!
365 multiply by the times I took pleasures of wanting to forget that which stained my spirit.

A little pleasure with a little fear in my heart,
I took solace in church services attended 24/7.
365 he preached but never saw my stained spirit!

You knew me too well but never exposed me to the world.
Your rod world hit me hard every single night.
I never showed them my bruised and buttered skin.

I kept it between the three of us.
You, me and the shadow that hangs on the wall,
It taught me to pray in private and worship and praise out loud!

Broken and bruised!
Fragmented and buttered!
All year round, years took turns to fold, shake, and crash my soul.

Now you show your face
At last....
But still my sealed lips wish to ask you this...

Where have you been?

Him and Her

He smiles because she smiles.
Red roses she could smell the scent from miles.
Love harder say you love me countless times.
Love letters she has piles.
Primroses with a shinny skin that never pails.
A heart that never wails,
A seed he planted, she natured, he watered till they harvested and named it after the promise they made.
Paint our future colorless for it only awaits to be made.
Dreams of a lion and lioness she has dreamt till they labeled her a mad woman.
Love is in the air why stop when there is more wool to weave a beautiful world.
Loops and hoops!
Hooks and crooks!
Stop for a minute I have lost myself in you.
Other hearts preach love is scarce.
They scream our souls now starve to death.
He gives her plenty, she gives him a handful.
Surplus to give away to the world,
What you give is what you receive.

I feel love

Pink dress, red lips, kisses me.
The night is young so are we.
Big hips, firm breasts, please me.
The earth is round so am I.

Under the peach tree the pastor preached,
True love comes once in a blue moon; don't lose the moon whilst you count the stars.
On the ocean floor with souls and spirits that believe in love.
He led a choir that sang our song.

Under the crescent moon with a heart in his hand,
He flipped page after page.
I saw letters written in a pattern,
When he discovered a blank page,
That's when the pen asked it for a hand in marriage.

He preached he tamed many silver hearts.
Mine is golden so that's why he hasn't forgotten.
Under the sea lives a cobbler,
Our love is like a broken boot at times,
But it shall heal with time.

Furnace!

Your love is fire my heart it devours.
On top of the mountain where there are fountains of endless love springs.
Your love is the purest of springs let my spirit drink its thirst off.

Ours

I see happiness lingering in the shadows of a smile.
Only if I had the power to read your mind,
Then I could see through the pages of your thoughts if I had a place in your life sentence.
Every heartbeat confesses to the soul,
Deep inside a voice calls on your name trust me I only thought it was my mind playing games,
Is this all I need?
Must be a sign on the walls of my mind because I see you when I close my eyes,
The sound of your voice brings a smile to my heart.
The stars envy how I love you, even the night loathes my loving you,
for forever I shall be yours.
Even the stars in your eyes confirm this is heavenly alignment.
Love how the brightest star in my constellation is. Lips eclipse in the bliss of a kiss.
Your soul is what I seek, to write my name on your lips,
Your heart I shall have to keep, forever mine, I shall guard it like the devil's layer,
It's never to be for the world to torment,
I shall torture you with love I shall, till you bleed not of hatred, but trust, patience, faithfulness and kindness
And the trust patience, faithfulness and kindness shall weave together.
Like a piece of royal fabric,
And we shall wear this love like a perfume until the end of time.
And the trust patience, faithfulness and trust shall weave us
Like a piece of royal fabric.

And we shall wear this love like a perfume till the end of time into eternity.
Fear not for I shall ride with you.

COLORLESS RAINBOW

Ecstatic sounds pimped wine.
Broken tables we dine.
I with the emerald dime,
For tomorrow hides it's prime.
No pain no gain!
No love no pain!
No joy no memory!
Let mine erase the melodies.
Joy remains not in memory.

Fill my glass.
Burn colorless paintings,
Fill the class.
Burn fruitless teachings,

Never forget the pain.
Send them off to never land on a crane.
So it remains as young as the sour spring.
Happy thoughts, tears they bring.

Happy moments fly on a plane.
To a deep dense forest to reign,
Not a soul ever lived there.

Waste land is the island.
Once a spotless rob,
Now a dotted clock!
Hour hand strikes o'clock,
Clueless bird, it tick tocks.

Don't you follow the mob?
Wind and I play ping pong.
Foggy it seemed back and forth on the see-saw swing.
Grey clouds sing song.

Back and forth we waltz.
Cast a glance at the walls.
Closing in with rhythmic calls,
Into the deep my hearts falls.

We tango without a clue.
Mocking jay whispered it's due.
Night gives birth to the morning dew.
Will you whisper I do?

It won't hurt as we bleed.
Arrogantly never plead,
This dance makes us forget the pain.
Beautiful is the colorless rainbow we paint.

True to the heart
Clessy & Live soul

Let not your eye be the enemy to what might last forever.
For the eye only blinks countless times when it meets that which bling.
Trust, not all that glitter is gold!

What is essential is invincible to the eye.
It is only with the heart that one may choose rightly.
For what attracts the heart is more than what the eye can see.
It is beyond the eye and the mind.
Greater than the connection of souls and spirits,
Truth only lies deep within the heart.
For the tongue lies so please stay true to the heart for we only have but just a little.
Time it flies.

We can love a little

I would rather drawn in your heart than in the pool of roses.
And swim in your eyes than the moonlight's orgies.
Still feel the wetness of your lips whenever my mind closes and I still feel there is never to be any to jump over all these gorges.
I wanna die in your arms so your kiss will be my resurrecting reason.
For the sound of your name to be my second life's reason!
Never shall I be jealous of the river's commitment, how he cherishes the marble stone, trust me she once told of her love diaries, how the river has taken her far and wide for I know you have captured the moon and the stars to decorate my heart and now it's ever shining because of your love.
Kiss me, Hide me in your warmth and let time miss me.
Mend this broken vessel and complete me.
The taste of your breath and breast birth wings beneath me.
Make me believe I will make you a king, believe me I will give you a promotion.
For what's a king without his Queen? Life without you is torture.
Too long I've toiled in.
I've searched the firmament.
Madness felt permanent.
Asked the heavens for you and they replied they've never seen
Such beauty unmatched!
Our souls can never be mismatched.
Set your hand in mine.
Abduct this heart of mine.
Let the stars align.
You and I together nothing more divine,
Whisper me a symphony as our tongues intertwine.

I'll sip from your every pore forever your love is the fairest of wine.
Please don't save me dear knight when I drawn in your heart,
Let your love choke me to death, to die in the pleasures for your touch I treasure Refuse me nil.
Diffuse into me till.
Like a solid lake we're still.
Burn the seven seas for you I will.
Let me play a piano on your skin.
As you arch your back and I live under your skin.
Never stop till you can't go on more, give me your all and the springs shall be yours.
How can I stop?
The tightness between your thighs leaves me no hope,
But to surrender.
Stroke your other tongue till I shudder.
Star spangled sky we lay under.
Glued by sweat let my tongue goes yonder.
Deeper is my love's keeper until your spring's rain...
Can we love again...?

Dodo

Bride's maid at my own wedding!
Granny's pee, call it peach tea.
Broken stranger at my own funeral!
Fly away flightless bird, fly.

Paddled the canoe with hands!
Rough waters, no coxswain has overcome.
Concubine in my own bedroom!
Fly away flightless fly.

Leer at that amaranth at the center of your heart.
Play ludo with refined harlots.
Covet for the title courtesan.
Fly flightless bird, fly.

Let mine lurch at the lich gate.
A bottle of exotic liqueur for the gods!
Made intelligence account for my struggle,
Fly away flightless bird fly.

Mine intend to extirpate the jester.
Betterhalf in conjunction with mistress destruction,
A coup d'état of conjugal restoration,
Fly away flightless bird fly.

Lip reading was never the fashion for men to wear.
Body language is all they understand.
Full moon right over our heads,

A damsel stands like an amphora on a dining table.
Dressed in lace, make soldiers go gaga.
Feed on bullets, mesmerized by the harlot's fashion.
Lips painted red ivy.
A glance casted, it runs to embrace mother cobra.

I was left hanging on.
Every cold night I wished on.
In my death bed, two shadows on the walls was me and you.
In real life it was you and her.

Lingerie, see through linen,
Leaving well curved frames for your eyes to see,
Like a gazelle leap into your arms.
Covet his finger prints on my lingerie.

Winter sun left mine in distress.
In the dark soul dies slowly,
No cry, kneel like a ewe before the guillotine.
The dodo bird longs for the flight to the moon in his arms.

To die alone in his eyes,
When will you learn to fly alone?
Fly away, flightless bird fly!

Virgin Mary

She plays a violin,
He never bothers to sing along to it.
When she cries he baths in her tears.
Disturbed by her laugher,
He prays she bleeds,
Keep bleeding Virgin Mary; keep bleeding, for you are no more
You are Nothing compared to his ladies of the night,
Virgin Mary lost the battle, Virgin Mary failed the test, and Virgin Mary is now like the rest.
Like there is no such thing as a black Christmas,
Virgin Mary is just another fairy tale in an old book the unknown author wrote.
He stole her diamond the one she had kept for long.
No one will believe her if she tells her story,
At least her diary knows her well.
At least in that book that's where her soul feels at home.
Virgin Mary with no hope!!!

Only survivor

The candle slowly burns.
The ashes slowly turn to dust.
The life in the roses is slowly fading.
So is my shell!

Prescribed, prescriptions, capsules,
I watched every little fur fall off,
Skeletons became visible.
One…..two…

Find out what it is not,
Before we know what it is!
Tubes, needles, gloves,
Men with dust coats,
Nothing! They found nothing.

By the veranda it sat,
Watching the fading sun,
The world only seems beautiful when we are about to leave it!
Beautiful when the sun shades its last rays!

It barked not.
Only last night the moon was full,
It shed a tear.
It rained a few drops.
A rainbow at midnight,
It bid me farewell!

No Heart Beat

Rivers flow none stop.
Water so clear and pure just like a new born baby's soul,
That is when I saw stepping stones to paradise.
I see the blue sky right above us.
I fell in love with your outside.

But I didn't know what was inside till we brought your inside outside.
Now Rivers stopped flowing and the forest died.
Mother Nature was troubled.
Our love was fire.

I see grey clouds right above us.
It's about to rain a storm of fire is coming.
I fell in love with your outside.
I didn't know what was inside till we brought your inside outside.

Rivers flow, Rivers stopped flowing,
The forest died slowly, just like how my heart stopped beating.
Blood ties

At the corner of the bed I sat.
I dreamt I was a Queen.
I dreamt he was a king.
He was a knight, everything I ever wanted.

Now he was right there.
I felt no connections.
But he said we are, were love.

Like oil in water, my heart floated.
Then I felt I had blood clotted in my veins.
Then the angel of death was sent to take my soul.

Trapped in the visions I see a web you created.
I can't breathe but still I find happiness in my dreams.
The world I created.
Not because of this love we thought we had.
Not because of the love I thought I had.
But because of the bond I thought we had.
Worst fears
Stab my heart right to the core
Let's fake our love just like the faked sounds I hear when we make love.
Pretend to fly like eagles when we only falling from the tree top.
We both know our feathers we burnt in winter.
Let's enjoy the pain when we hit the rough rocky ground, let's act like
It's the only thing we know about falling in love.
Confess you love me kiss me on the cheek like Judas.
Like the devil tears define hatred.
You only weep when your heart is at peace.
Snake! Your love is poison and my heart,
Spirit and soul you have captured in a little cage.
I'm a bird with no feathers,
Tell me to jump so that in your heart I die slowly.
You say focused, can't you see I can barely stand in your eyes, I'm crawling.
Crooked is your smile, I can see beyond it.
I know you wish me well and so do I.
You are my life line!!!

Will you make the death wish quicker?
Can't you see my soul has grown old; I'm struggling to keep up.
Piece of a broken heart

Fragmented is thy soul,
Unturned like a stone but badly wounded is thy heart,
It's useless to think hard,
As I try to ponder to see yonder,
Beyond lies the question to this life,
How to solve this puzzle,
My heart bleeds for internal love,
My soul pleads not for mislead,
Still fail to please in this displease of an unsolved quiz,
At no time to be found as I hide in the shadows of a beautiful smile

All that's left

All that's left of us
Are these faded pictures on the wall?
Love left us decades ago
All that's left of us now is the hate I can tell by the look in your eyes

Remember me so I remember you so we remember us
Look at the clock; look at how the time has passed
Stone cold war hearts, bitter sweet love trust in lies
Kiss not my lips I prefer the cheeks, my forehead says there is no trust but you trust it means trust between us both so you still trust

Dreams fade no more you and me
Trees wither as our love reaches the peek
Please keep up how I can breathe when you, my lifelines, have abandoned me
Please breathe love I can feel the hate in the air, can't you feel the breeze
My heart freeze you, breathe a heavy storm, please make it stronger for my heart to burst quicker

Your words are thicker so I pray in them, I drown quicker
They say blood is thick but love is thicker, what's left is nothing but muddy water I pray we sink in quicker

As we go down the river
Look at the rocks, they
Are getting bigger
A crack on this boat I see us sinking

So love, breathe in slowly
This might be your last
For long shall we last?
I know God knows that you know what my heart knows so I know where your mind goes every single time I hit the wrong notes
Please take note of these signs when the boat goes down the river
So does our souls in this I surrender you are the winner
But know this, I tried so you tried and God tried to hold us together through this rocky ride
So fare well, don't you cry I know you know that I'm forever smiling even though my heart will be crying
You will never see me crawling even though we both know I'm a cripple,
 Love we blame and so it controlled me

Don't

When the sun goes down and I'm not home yet
When the shadows of the trees get over shadowed by the dark sad night
Remember this; I'm just a lost lonely cold iron hearted soul with a faded spirit

I never vowed to love for eternity
I only took you in as an orphan and so there is no "we"
I only donate the truth to the lost souls
Whose spirits deny "there is no love in the air just lust?"

I don't have the heart
I don't have the soul and spirit
My life depends not on love,
So don't look for me when I'm gone

Kisses are just kisses and there is no hidden meaning in between
Romance is a nightmare that kills you in your sleep if you are never careful
I never mean things that I say,
Doubt my Innocent eyes, I'm a
Monster

Most hearts been buried,
Most souls have perished,
Please stay away I'm not the one you should trust
I'm never gentle,
In the love realm they call me a psycho
Don't miss me too much!!!

Remember Me

Watch the sunset....
The sand is glad to have you take a walk

Feel the wind blow.....
The trees are glad to have you sit a while among them

Take some time to look back.....
The years are glad to have carried you this far without me

Sing along to old broken songs.....
The birds are glad to hear your broken voice

Years go by...
A year feels like two minutes in your world
The time is glad to keep racing till our memories are forgotten

My shadow pleads with the present to never erase the past,
Even though it holds nothing but tears, pain and sorrow

'Burn them not to ashes'
'Bury them not in the deepest cave'
'Although your ears miss not the sound of her voice'
'she only asks you to remember her'

Remember me...
Like a shadow our memories linger in my heart

Salty waters flow endlessly on the thought of you

The rusty landline, now a home for the roaches
I left a thousand tears, now the salty waters no longer flow on the thought of the lady bird

I know you have been praying for changes
Tired of.....
A thousand times we kept going through these phases

Poured you a crunch of bitter wine
With a smile you sipped on
Late night I saw your shadow crying
The pavement whispered
'your wine is too bitter to swallow'

Even though now the years seem to be narrow
I pray your memories of me don't become shallow

I now sing.....
'Faded pictures hang'
'In neatly netted webs they hang'
'Friends with the eight legs monsters I am'
'The dusty glitters spackle'

You hardly smiled....
I made you swallow the bitter honey
Even though the memory of us brings tears and pain
Always go back to that day when we first met
Will you smile and remember me...?

I do

There are not more than a million words
A few said with not much effort
Your tongue used to struggle but now it's used to it
Your lips they used to struggle but now they are used to it

That which is of the essence can never be seen with a naked eye
Only those gifted with the eyesight to see beyond the twinkle of an eye
But to hear and see the throbbing of a heart beat
And a heart that speaks a foreign language that even the most educated find complicated

Words Unspoken off
Back then it felt like I was stripping my mouth naked
Found my lips being sealed though my heart was about to burst with zeal

I did pray if they were all lies then my tongue should get thwarted
Although my heart dances and sings
My eyes twinkle and twinkle in a frivolous way
I fumbled my way to the centre of your heart
Gobbled all the lies you fake love - generously courted and wrapped up
Drama king I only do have three words for you
I do care

Listen

I made you my all.
In the darkest night in your arms I would fall.
In the coldest days in your heart I found a home.
Your words made me whole.

In complete was the name our neighbours used to call.
You came and rubbed it off.
I have never felt so much joy,
Unlike Romeo and Juliet from your love I would never choke.

From a heart that of a crow my heart swims on the ocean floor,
To the heart that of a swan my heart bleeds for more,
I am for you and you are for me, won't you sing along with me?
Let's write a song on this solid fountain of love together and
forever it shall live in our hearts.

My soul used to preach of the love that hurts,
The love that crushes and burns your spirit,
The love that makes you choke to death,
The love that has no hearts in it, no emotions to it just minds filled lust.

Now that I found you I swear I won't let you go.
I wouldn't want to be caught singing the blues.
Now that you found me, I swear to make every second count.
I wouldn't want to be caught preaching about the one that got away.
Understand I am for you and you are for me.

I can be all you ever wanted.

I fall too hard that's my weakness.
I can be all you ever dreamt of, a Cinderella with a caring heart and high spirited.
I can easily drawn in your words but they better not be lies,
Because baby I can be the worst.
I can easily become a monster, I won't hesitate to tear you apart, watch you burn down to ashes.
It will all be in the name of love so please do not cross the road when it red light blinks.

Stand By

He came in with a smile on his face.
His shadow resembled the devil himself.
The stupid naive little girl chose to be blind.
Now she waits by the river hoping the Spirits might give her a vision.

She took his hand with a smile on her face.
Her shadow trembled with fear.
The Smart old joker chose to be blind.
Now he giggles with the dark shadows,
Got a hand shake from the snake,
A pat on the back for a job well done,
What a well-played match mate!

Stand by the river.
The water spirits will show you a vision,
The man was a snake,
The gods in the wind showed you his companion
"The shadow"
Foolish girl should be burnt to ashes,
You are a disgrace to all the mothers.
How dare you fall blind!
You looked aside when the great spirits showed you the essentials.

Stand by in the desert.
Maybe the desert gods might show you tombs of ancient naive little girls,
Whose life ended in the name of love?
Love led them to the grave,

Look back at Romeo and Juliet you foolish idiot.
How dare you trust a heart with a beard?

Stand by in the woods.
Maybe Mother Nature might come to your rescue,
'I have given up on you', the inner me wrote.
His words poisoned many souls,
I love you means I want you.
Croaked smile more like a half moon smile of an evil one.
How come you chose to be blind?
Where you desperate for love?
To be loved?

Stand by for now.
God will send a true lover.
It might take ages,
But for you he shall cross oceans.
For now stand by!

LET IT GO

In a corner I sat
Hands folded my heart bleeds not I don't feel the pain,
Not anymore and so here I am tonight I shall sing.
Let it go!
Let it go!
Let it go soon you will grow then glow

Yes think no more of it
Let it float yes like a raft
Just dance and sing till your throat gets sores
Jump up and down, Move from left to right
Let it go soon you will grow then glow

Under the shade I stood
Hands in the air, my heart hurts not
I don't hate you, not anymore
And so here I am tonight I shall scream
Swing my hands, Yes node my head
Feel the rhythm, yes get carried away
Just sing and dance till your legs get numb
Let it go soon you will grow then glow!!

Never

I'm never going to cry.
I have cried an ocean decades ago.
My tears are way too precious than gold.
Why waste them on a priceless moulding of clay like you?
Seriously! I have other things to do,
Smiling is one of them.
If I can't be laughing with you then I shall laugh with my neighbour's dog.
And one thing that is for sure is never in my life will I ever be blue over a crazy, stupid and selfish being like you.
Believe me I have had it with your kind!
Sly back stabbing - frown whilst they are not looking and smile in their face so they don't get what's cooking kind of creatures.
I swear if I was a god of thunder I could have zapped you from the face of the earth maybe banish you for all eternity.
Thank your so called gods I never got the chance to possess a time machine,
I could have re-winded it back to when you were in your mother's womb.
I could have poisoned her drink so instead of giving birth to such a hideous being,
She could have flashed you down the toilet drain or maybe vomited you back to the soil where you belong.
Aar!
Just so you should know,
Never in my life would I ever be blue over you!

Come by the tree

Come by the tree.
A grave I dig for our deceased hearts to bury.
Are you coming to the tree where the crescent moon hangs?
Now my soul grows wary,
I feel inside my heart burns.
End it now or forever these walls shall stand.
A cupid with an arrow to strike your heart I send.
Tell the truth to shame the night; where do we stand?
Forever yours or never to be the ones whose souls blend?

Will you come by the river where the sand is thicker?
Put on that velvet garment I will make it quicker.
Put an end to us both, don't you think but run if you can't keep up.
I walk still in the same road hoping one day you shall fall back and follow.
Words I have not for my lips you have sealed.
Shame on you!
Coward! You drew back without me,
What goes around comes back around.

Next fall I won't meet you half way.
You shall preach about the one that got away.
Join me as I watch the mountains fall,
Help me light up the tree where the crescent moon hangs.
Help me make the wind blow harder so it burns.

PUBLIC TOILET

She got used I'm telling you!
Like a toilet paper in a public toilet she is now an empty lose canon.
Every man in the town have either used her as a face towel,
Broom, dust pan or harrow you name it.
Old poor used up self,
You can run but you can't hide from the shame
You should have known your worth an tagged it
They now talk of you like a soccer player
They now look at you in disgust, you should have known,
They don't love you, but they would love to use you till you worn out.
Pale skin, no more oily black hair Curves gone, mashed potato like breasts
Ebony skin six fit under –buried
Burden your mother with another mouth to feed,
Will you ever learn from your mistakes?
Men lie that's a fact!
Don't be fooled, to drink their thirst from every river is what they ever know.

Primrose

Once upon a song,
The wind used to play me that love song,
Back then when rain was courting me.

Once upon a rain drop fell in love with a primrose,
Ever since their first kiss she has always bloomed,
Bright as the sun she shone in her days.

The wind became jealous,
And so did the sand,
That's when the cyclone alliance was formed.

Let us destroy rain once and for all,
That's what they swore.
Primrose lost her bright smile.

Primrose had no lover.
Love meant nothing to her by then it was just like the dark days.
She envied the marble stone when she told her love diaries.

How the river cherishes her and travels with her all around the world.
How he would never abandon her,
If he was to die they would die together.

She envied the moon and how she fell for the star,
Their bound is forever unshakeable,
And how beautiful they look together,

And forever they shall remain a part of each other.
Rain drop was never strong to stand his ground,
He got defeated, Sand and wind always had their ways.

No matter how strong he seemed,
He always got blown in another direction,
He always lost to them.

Primrose, how can you fall for rain drop?
He comes and goes.
Leaves you to die!

He aint yours for the keeping,
Poor Primrose!
Open your eyes I will help you see!

What belongs to you will always stay,
Just like the meadow he never leaves,
Primrose, when you will see the love I have for you.

Don't search hard and reach out too far,
For what you seek might be right under your nose.

Purpose

Oh Lord, dear Lord taking every word in.
I swallow the pill every single day,
I have prayers written down in rows and columns.
On the walls, on the ceiling and I craved them on the floor too.
You know I can never say them,
My lips have been sealed for years.
I have thousands of sins committed all in 24hours multiply by my age.
My colours are red and black,
Black blend with my heart, my spirit and soul,
Black is the blood that I write prayers with on the walls.
My skin is covered in red,
Red little letters that say you shall burn.
My right hand is curved with an iron pin little fleshy words that say
  'repent you serpent'
What is my purpose?
To serve like a little demon that destroys hearts?
What is my purpose and destiny?

Oh Lord God!!
I love them all; I'm obsessed with them all,
I can never get enough.
Peter is kind, Johnny is tall, Joseph is rich, and I just can't decide, who I should be with?
Lord! Your word on adultery, your word on Lust, Your word on harlotry,
It has fallen on deaf ears.
Hosea and his harlot, Am I the second version of her?

Who can be the Hosea?
Prudence!
He knows about them all, he knows my heart is divided,
And I'm a woman of purity but still walk in the shadows of the woman that rule the night.
 Fate and destiny!
Who am I?
 What is my purpose and destiny?
To have whosoever I please and still be labelled the prophetess?

DESTINY

Destined to love,
Yet I hate.
Destined to cherish these moments,
Yet I loathe them.
It rains, yes for decades it shall.
I hate the mud but I love the smell of wet soil.
I hate the strong winds but I love how they ripple through my clothes.

Blank Pages

I sat down deep in thoughts,
Reminiscing of how the black book became so colourful.
Was it your heart that sang the rainbow song?
Was it your love that wrote colourful patterns in mine?

Blank pages, are all that's left of the poor book.
Blank pages, the colourful lyrics abandoned.
Blank pages, I flipped on hoping to find the remains.
Remains to the promises we made over night.

Emptiness now rules in my heart,
Loneliness I have crowned the king of my heart,
Hatred is the only feeling ever known to my heart,
Ever since we parted ways, the pages have been falling out since then.

And now I'm a blank page with no purpose.
I'm a blank page the ink divorced.
I feel worthless!
The fire refused to burn me to dust.

The wind ripples not through me,
I only wish to be exposed to total destruction and doom,
For your heart that sang the rainbow song is six feet under,
For your love that painted colourful patterns in mine is no longer in the air.

You shall be forever missed and remain in memory.

But these blank pages, who shall draw colourful patterns in them?
I pray for the time to fly fast,
I live not now my spirit is long gone and my soul is longing for our reunion.

I only await my hour,
So I can be reunited with you, painter of hearts and author to blank books,
So we can sing our book back to life again.

In and out

Think not child,
Your brains will explode.
Scream not from the inside child,
Let it out.
Breathe in and out.

Be up and stressing no more my dear child.
Your brains are way too young and pretty for such an adventure,
I know you and the world share a dark chapter.
I can smell the deodorant of fear that drips like droplets of water from your armpits.
But breathe in and out,
Count backwards and count again till you forget that which upsets you.

The world is a beautiful place, but you must know it also has its dark shadows.
Black and white, evil and good,
The balance between the two has to be maintained.
So when the shadows creep in,
Sing that song,
"The light over comes darkness, I am pure you shall not touch me."

Every dog shall have its own day,
And so remember patience pays, write it on your forehead "P2"
Tattoo it in your brains "PP" or the double "P's" in case you might forget
Right before meeting any decisions,
Always breathe in and out,

Anger is that of the impure.

Forgiving and forgetting,
How other souls have wronged you brings joy to the heart.
Never let anger take control in your life,
You might slip and bite your tongue instead.
Words can hurt than a heavy beating,
Take it from me child; I only wish for you to become the second better me.

So whenever you feel you are about to burst and spurs,
Breathe in and out or you might hurt a precious spirit.

16

Please love me better!
Please hold me right there!
Please save me!
Save me old man, sit under the Muhacha tree every single night,
They want a Virgin,
She is pure you know,
She has never known a man before.

Mug after mug!
I can handle the burning sensation.
I've been drinking brew since I was a foetus in my mother's womb.
Who doesn't know me? Even the elderly men in the village,
I danced to the drum and the mbira they played,
Dust like smoke it raised,
The trees coughed so hard they will never forget this day.

Ask them they know my name,
In the river where I bathed away tears of joy,
Struggle, love, hate and trust me it knows my Surname.
16 and innocent!

He drove off!
She had made a lot!
God given beauty,
Curves that resemble the most beautiful mountains in Inyanga,
Skin brown as the soil in Mutoko,
Hair black as ebony,
Flawless, Flawless!

Even the night cannot deny it,
She is beautiful.
Only Old, grown, mature, respected, rich, sick, arrogant man
Wearing expensive perfumes know of her beauty.
Beauty that shames the beautiful roses,
Bottle after bottle, she consumed.
Oooh! The burning sensation
16 and innocent!

Please love me better!
My heart is still growing in love,
Please hold me right there.
Appreciate me!
Please I'm only 16 and innocent!
What is love?

Blue

In the blue ocean I shall swim,
Wash away all my sins,
So under the blue sky I sore free.

What if water is life?
What if this life ends sooner?
What if blue means light?
Will it be the one that shall last forever?
What if blue means long life?

The endless blue sky smiles
'There is no end'
The eagle, the king of the sky failed to meet it,
And the clouds sang
'This God is Greater'
'He is the creator'

Blue oceans flow endlessly,
Water is life supposedly,
I was the eagle flying aimlessly,
To see where this blue sky ends roughly,
I thought there was wall on the other end of this semi-circle more like a ball plastered with blue cement.

I flew to the East, the West, the North, and the South,
Then I flew South West, South East, North East, and North West,
Then concluded the only thing thy feet can ever feel is the ground and seas.

What if blue means endless life?
What if the endless blue sky is telling a story of what is to come?
What if the blue Oceans and blue Seas are telling a story of what the next life is going to be like?
No Dying or Crying!

What if blue means an endless ribbon to immortality, flawless, and blameless life?
What if the stillness of the blue Oceans and Seas resemble the peace that is going to be bestowed upon us all in the next life?
What if the clear blue sky resembles the flawlessness of the soul and spirit that is to come on the morrow?

I said what if the unstableness of the blue Oceans, Seas
And the rumbling of thunder and lightning bolts resemble God's anger and the dying rivers resemble the end of time?
What if the grey clouds bury the blue sky forever and the blue oceans turn to pitch black?

What if it is already too late to turn back?

But Remember this!!

The ocean is blue!
Water is life!
And so blue means life?

The sky is blue!
Let's paint your life blue.
So blue means an endless life in the next life?

Why not cherish blue instead?
Why not take hid of these signs, for we are living in an age where everything has a hidden meaning.
Blue!

Mmap New African Poets Series

If you have enjoyed *Ethiopian Aliens*, consider these other fine books in the **Mmap New African Poets Series** from *Mwanaka Media and Publishing*:

I Threw a Star in a Wine Glass by Fethi Sassi
Best New African Poets 2017 Anthology by Tendai R Mwanaka and Daniel Da Purificacao
Logbook Written by a Drifter by Tendai Rinos Mwanaka
Mad Bob Republic: Bloodlines, Bile and a Crying Child by Tendai Rinos Mwanaka
Zimbolicious Poetry Vol 1 by Tendai R Mwanaka and Edward Dzonze
Zimbolicious Poetry Vol 2 by Tendai R Mwanaka and Edward Dzonze
Zimbolicious: An Anthology of Zimbabwean Literature and Arts, Vol 3 by Tendai Mwanaka
Under The Steel Yoke by Jabulani Mzinyathi
Fly in a Beehive by Thato Tshukudu
Bounding for Light by Richard Mbuthia
Sentiments by Jackson Matimba
Best New African Poets 2018 Anthology by Tendai R Mwanaka and Nsah Mala
Words That Matter by Gerry Sikazwe
The Ungendered by Delia Watterson
Ghetto Symphony by Mandla Mavolwane
Sky for a Foreign Bird by Fethi Sassi
A Portrait of Defiance by Tendai Rinos Mwanaka
Zimbolicious: An Anthology of Zimbabwean Literature and Arts, Vol 4 by Tendai Mwanaka and Jabulani Mzinyathi

When Escape Becomes the only Lover by Tendai R Mwanaka
ويَسهَرُ اللَّيلُ عَلى شَفَتي...وَالغَمَام by Fethi Sassi
A Letter to the President by Mbizo Chirasha
This is not a poem by Richard Inya
Pressed flowers by John Eppel
Righteous Indignation by Jabulani Mzinyathi:
Blooming Cactus by Mikateko Mbambo
Rhythm of Life by Olivia Ngozi Osouha
Travellers Gather Dust and Lust by Gabriel Awuah Mainoo
Chitungwiza Mushamukuru: An Anthology from Zimbabwe's Biggest Ghetto Town by Tendai Rinos Mwanaka
Zimbolicious: An Anthology of Zimbabwean Literature and Arts, Vol 5 by Tendai Mwanaka
Because Sadness is Beautiful? by Tanaka Chidora
Of Fresh Bloom and Smoke by Abigail George
Shades of Black by Edward Dzonze
Best New African Poets 2020 Anthology by Tendai Rinos Mwanaka, Lorna Telma Zita and Balddine Moussa
This Body is an Empty Vessel by Beaton Galafa
Between Places by Tendai Rinos Mwanaka
Best New African Poets 2021 Anthology by Tendai Rinos Mwanaka, Lorna Telma Zita and Balddine Moussa
Zimbolicious: An Anthology of Zimbabwean Literature and Arts, Vol 6 by Tendai Mwanaka and Chenjerai Mhondera
A Matter of Inclusion by Chad Norman
Keeping the Sun Secret by Mariel Awendit
سِجلٌّ مَكتُوبٌ لتَانِهِ by Tendai Rinos Mwanaka
Ghetto Blues by Tendai Rinos Mwanaka
Zimbolicious: An Anthology of Zimbabwean Literature and Arts, Vol 7 by Tendai Rinos Mwanaka and Tanaka Chidora

Best New African Poets 2022 Anthology by Tendai Rinos Mwanaka and Helder Simbad
Dark Lines of History by Sithembele Isaac Xhegwana
a sky is falling by Nica Cornell
Death of a Statue by Samuel Chuma
Along the way by Jabulani Mzinyathi
Strides of Hope by Tawanda Chigavazira
Young Galaxies by Abigail George
Coming of Age by Gift Sakirai
Mother's Kitchen and Other Places by Antreka. M. Tladi
Best New African Poets 2023 Anthology by Tendai Rinos Mwanaka, Helder Simbad and Gerald Mpesse
Zimbolicious Anthology Vol 8 by Tendai Rinos Mwanaka and Mathew T Chikono
Broken Maps by Riak Marial Riak
Formless by Raïs Neza Boneza
Of poets, gods, ghosts. Irritants and storytellers by Tendai Rinos Mwanaka

Soon to be released

In The Inferno by Jabulani Mzinyathi

www.ingramcontent.com/pod-product-compliance
Lightning Source LLC
Chambersburg PA
CBHW070848160426
43192CB00012B/2354